Indian Nations

THE NAVAJO

by
Lana T. Griffin and Tommy J. Nockideneh

General Editors
Herman J. Viola and Felix C. Lowe

A Rivilo Book

RSVP
**RAINTREE
STECK-VAUGHN**
P U B L I S H E R S
A Steck-Vaughn Company

Austin, Texas

www.steck-vaughn.com

Published by Raintree Steck-Vaughn Publishers, an imprint of the Steck-Vaughn Company

Developed for Steck-Vaughn Company by Rivilo Books, Bluffton, SC
Editor: Jan Danis
Photo Research: William A. Eames and Paula Dailey
Design: Barbara Lisenby and Todd Hirshman
Electronic Preparation: Curry Printing

Raintree Steck-Vaughn Publishers Staff
Publishing Director: Walter Kossmann
Editor: Kathy DeVico
Design Project Manager: Lyda Guz

Photo Credits: Lana T. Griffin: cover; pp. 7, 8, 9, 13, 15, 20, 21 top, 22, 24, 25, 27, 28, 32, 36 right, 38, 40, 41; Lisa Ranallo Horse Capture: illustration, pp. 4, 6; Paul Chesley/NGS Image Collection: p. 10; ©Ilka Hartmann: pp. 11, 24 right, 35; ©Arthur Shilstone, 1997: p. 14; Corbis/Bettmann–UPI: p. 17; Weavings from the Maxwell Museum of Anthropology of the University of New Mexico painted by Ned Seidler/NGS Image Collection: p. 18; Terry Eiler: pp. 19 left, 33; Smithsonian Anthropological Archives: pp. 19 right, 21 bottom, 24 left, 26, 30; Library of Congress: pp. 23, 29; Michéle Brinson: illustration, p. 31 left; Victor Boswell/NGS Image Collection: p. 31 right; U.S. Marine Corps: p. 34; Bruce Dale/NGS Image Collection: pp. 36 left, 42, 43; Richard Clarkson/NGS Image Collection: p. 37; David A. Harvey/NGS Image Collection: p. 39.

Library of Congress Cataloging-in-Publication Data
Griffin, Lana T.
    The Navajo/Lana T. Griffin and Tommy J. Nockideneh.
      p.   cm — (Indian nations)
    "A Rivilo book."
    Includes bibliographical references and index.
    ISBN 0-8172-5463-3
    1. Navajo Indians — History — Juvenile literature.
    2. Navajo Indians — Social life and customs — Juvenile literature.   I. Nockideneh, Tommy J. II. Title. III. Series.
    E99.N3G92 2000   98-42351
    979.1'004972 — dc21   CIP

Printed and bound in the United States of America
1 2 3 4 5 6 7 8 9 0 LB 03 02 01 00 99

Contents

How Coyote Stole Fire

When the First People came to the Fifth World and the four seasons were established, some of the time it was too hot, and some of the time it was too cold. Even Coyote was cold in his home in Coyote Mountain. He wished that he had a spark of fire from Fire Man's Mountain to heat his house, but he was too lazy to go and get fire himself. He decided to convince another animal to do the work for him. But Badger wouldn't go. And Skunk wouldn't go. And Gopher wouldn't go. And Mole wouldn't even leave his house under the ground.

Coyote thought of the bird people, and they agreed to Coyote's plan. A bird would fly to the top of Fire Man's Mountain carrying a bundle of reeds. When the reeds caught fire, he would bring the flaming bundle back. Coyote forgot to say that Fire Man would shoot arrows at anyone trying to steal fire. And besides, monsters guarded the fire. Flicker flew to Fire Man's Mountain and tried to bring back fire, but the monsters burned his wings until they turned red. Hawk also tried but burned his tail red, too.

Finally Coyote himself went to the top of Fire Man's Mountain. He carried a bundle of reeds on his tail and salt crystals in his mouth. He also carried shells strung on seaweed. He tricked the monsters by telling them the shells were magic and would cool them off. Coyote asked to stand near the fire, and then he spit the salt from his mouth into the eyes of the monsters. Fire Man came up out of the fire pit to shoot arrows.

◀ Coyote brings fire to the First People.

5

He shot four burning arrows at Coyote, who caught them in the bundle of reeds on his tail. Coyote ran down the mountain very fast in a zigzag way.

At last Coyote arrived at the home of First Woman. He asked her to cut off the reeds so that his tail would stop burning. People quickly took the reeds, and they had fire for their homes. Coyote looked at his tail sadly. Once it had been white like Fox's tail, but now it was tipped with black. And so it is to this day.

✳ ✳ ✳

Coyote, Badger, and First Woman—these are familiar characters in Navajo stories. The animals and the **Holy People** appear over and over in the stories that explain how the world of the Navajos came to be the way it is.

Creation Story

The Navajo's name for themselves is the **Diné** (pronounced DIN eh). The story of the creation of the Diné and their world or homeland, called Dinetah (DIN eh TAH), has many parts and many versions. The stories are told again and again during the healing and blessing **ceremonies** of Navajo religious life. When they are retold within the family, the stories entertain and instruct adults and children. Knowledge about the world and moral lessons from the stories enrich daily life.

In one version of the creation story, there were four worlds before the present Fifth World. These worlds were populated by the insect and bat people, the bird people, the grasshopper people, humans, and the Holy People. Because humans and animal people were not able to get along with one another, they had to move from one world to the next.

Talking God and other Holy People created First Man and First Woman from two ears of corn. Wind gave them life.

*The ruins of Pueblo Bonito in Chaco Canyon, New Mexico. They were part of a large settlement that was abandoned by the **Anasazi** before the Navajo made their homes nearby.*

Spider Rock is said to be the ancient home of Spider Woman, who taught Navajo women how to weave.

Eventually First Man and First Woman emerged into the present world of Dinetah. Here they were taught how to build a **hogan** by Talking God and how to build a **sweat lodge** by Lightning. First Man and First Woman created Sun and Moon. They were hanging the stars in patterns when they were interrupted by impatient Coyote, who tossed the stars into the sky and formed the Milky Way. First Man and First Woman then created the Earth People and taught them to be human.

First Man and First Woman raised a child who became Changing Woman. Changing Woman was one of the most helpful of the Holy People. She organized the Diné into the first four **clans**. Her greatest gift to the earth and its people was the idea of **hózhó** (HO jz ho). Hózhó means beauty, harmony, and balance. The idea of hózhó is the center of Navajo religion.

Changing Woman had twin sons whose names were Monster Slayer and Child Born of Water. The twins discovered that their father was Sun. After they made a long journey to meet Sun, the brothers learned how to use their powers and became known as the Hero Twins. They killed many monsters that were living on the land. Signs of these battles can be found in rock formations throughout Dinetah.

All the animals have special talents in the creation stories of the Diné. Because they helped to settle the Fifth World, all creatures have an important place on the Earth, and all are to be respected.

Prehistory

In the creation story, it is explained that the Diné emerged from cold, dark worlds into a world of light and colors. And, in fact, the Navajos, along with the Apaches, came from a group of people who migrated from Asia about 10,000 years ago. They settled in what is now Alaska and northwestern Canada. Sometime between 800 and 1,100 years ago, small groups of

These petroglyphs, or drawings, of mountain goats were carved on a sandstone wall in Monument Valley many years ago.

these people began to leave their homes in the cold north. The travelers used dogs to carry loads and pull **travois** on their journey to their true homeland in the warm sunshine of the Southwest, in what is now New Mexico and Arizona.

Four sacred mountains mark the boundaries of Dinetah. Each is located in one of the four directions of the compass, and each stands for one of the four sacred colors: In the east is White Shell or Dawn (Mt. Blanca east of Alamosa, Colorado). In the south is Blue Bead or Turquoise (Mt. Taylor near Grants, New Mexico). In the west is Yellow Abalone Shell or Coral (San Francisco Peak near Flagstaff, Arizona). And in the north is Obsidian (Hesperus Peak west of Durango, Colorado). A Holy Person had circled this area to show that the people would be safe and protected there. The Diné settled in the canyons and mountains, and the high desert of the Southwest became their homeland.

Farmers dry corn in the open. Corn, beans, squash, and melons have long been principal crops for the Navajo.

From their neighbors, the **Pueblo** people, the Diné soon learned how to farm using only a little water. They planted corn, beans, squash, and melons. Growing crops allowed families to remain in one place for a long time, instead of constantly moving around to find food.

The Diné learned or improved their weaving of cloth from the Pueblo people. They also learned to make pottery and baskets. They became known as traders of cloth, meat, salt, and other minerals. By the time Spanish explorers arrived in the Southwest in the middle 1500s, the Diné were thriving.

Key Historical Events

Encounters with the Spanish

The Diné first met the Spanish and their horses in 1582 near Blue Bead (Mt. Taylor). The Spanish were searching for gold. Their leader, Antonio de Espejo, reported that the Navajo people brought food to the explorers.

In 1598 Juan de Oñate conquered the Pueblo and became governor of the Spanish settlement he called New Mexico. He brought sheep, goats, horses, and cattle and forced the Pueblo to care for them. The Diné raided the herds to capture the animals. Otherwise, they avoided the Spanish as much as possible.

At first the Spaniards confused the Diné with the Apaches, a related Athapaskan people. Spaniards called the Diné "Apaches de Nabajó," which they thought meant "Apaches of the planted fields." This is why they are called Navajos in English. In 1680 the Pueblos staged a revolt against the Spaniards and drove them out of the area. However, the Spaniards returned in 1692 to conquer the Pueblos. Many Pueblos fled from the Spaniards and were taken in by the Diné. Many similarities among Navajo and Pueblo customs and crafts come from this time.

Throughout the 1700s, few Navajos learned to speak Spanish, and even fewer attended the Catholic churches started by the **missionaries**. However, the Navajos did adopt plants and animals brought to the Southwest by Spanish priests and settlers. The Navajos began to grow fruits and vegetables such as peaches, wheat, and potatoes. Horses and sheep became especially important to the Navajo way of life.

Horses are loved by Navajo children today just as they were centuries ago.

Encounters with the United States

Warfare in the Southwest did not mean big battles. Small, fast raids were the usual pattern. Navajos and other nearby tribes, such as the Apaches and Utes, often raided each other. The Navajos also stole food, sheep, and horses from the New Mexicans. In retaliation, New Mexican settlers captured Navajo people to use as slaves. By the mid-1800s, about 5,000 to 6,000 Navajo slaves lived with New Mexican families.

This pattern of raiding continued until 1846, when the United States gained control of the Southwest during the Mexican-American War. Government agents tried to make written agreements called **treaties** with the Navajo **headmen**, who were leaders of small local groups. The agents mistakenly thought that the headmen were chiefs who could speak for large numbers of people.

The U.S. Army built Fort Defiance in the middle of Navajo country in 1851. A dispute over the murder of a slave owned by the fort's commander led to Army raids on the herds and fields of the Diné. Headmen Barboncito and Manuelito led about a thousand warriors in an attack on Fort Defiance. The U.S. Army, even with their more advanced weapons, barely won the battle.

In 1861 a group of Navajos came to the Army post Fort Fauntleroy to receive food as promised in a treaty. During an argument over a horse race, soldiers shot at the Navajos, killing several women and children. The Navajos raided white settlements in revenge.

Carleton and Carson on the Offensive

In 1863 the U.S. Army decided that the Navajos had to be brought under control. Brigadier General James Carleton came from California to lead the campaign. Carleton intended to round up all the scattered Navajos and Apaches and confine them near Fort Sumner, New Mexico. This area was called *Bosque Redondo*, which means "round hill" or "grove" in Spanish. Carleton's plan was for Bosque Redondo to be a reservation—a place to restrict the Diné and make them change their ways so that they would become "civilized" and act like Americans.

General Carleton chose Colonel Christopher "Kit" Carson to carry out his plans. Carson used a "scorched earth" policy. His troops were ordered to burn or destroy everything in their path. They burned hogans, laid waste to cornfields, and slaughtered sheep and horses. They killed people without warning.

Some Navajos surrendered, but many tried to escape by retreating farther into the canyons of Dinetah. Thousands hid in Canyon de Chelly (pronounced de SHAY). Soldiers followed them there and trapped them. Many Navajos starved to death during the long winter of 1863, and many others were shot by the soldiers. Finally, most of the survivors were captured. Still, some Navajos hid in other canyons and were never found.

Canyon de Chelly, in Arizona, has been inhabited for a thousand years or more. Many Navajo hid there in 1863 from Kit Carson and his men.

The Long Walk to Bosque Redondo

In March 1864 Carson and his troops rounded up scattered groups of captured Navajos and started them on their journey to their new home. The people were starving, and late blizzards caused additional hardships. Nevertheless, the Navajos were forced to march more than 350 miles (560 km) from Fort Defiance to Fort Sumner. Children and old people had trouble keeping up. Soldiers shot anyone who became ill or moved too slowly. Many people starved or froze to death on the way.

This terrible journey was known as "the Long Walk." Things did not get better for the people who managed to reach Bosque Redondo. The Diné called it *Hweeldi*, the Place of Despair. The people were forced to build barracks for the soldiers and houses for themselves. They had no blankets or clothes. There was no wood to build fires for cooking or heat. The water was salty and made many people sick. Irrigation ditches were dug, and seeds were planted—all without proper tools. Crops failed year after year because of drought, insects, or salty water. There was never enough to eat. Food that was shipped to the fort was stolen or arrived spoiled. A **smallpox** epidemic killed more than 2,000 people.

Throughout their ordeal the Navajos longed for Dinetah. The people loved their homeland and had strong ties to it through their creation stories. They continued to hold some of their ceremonies and to hope that the Holy People would help them.

In 1863 the Navajo were forced by Kit Carson and his troops to leave their homeland, but they returned five years later.

The Navajo Reservation

General Carleton's plan to "civilize" the Navajos was a complete failure. Some important citizens of New Mexico began to speak out about the cruel hardships at Bosque Redondo. In 1868 Carleton was replaced by William T. Sherman. The famous Civil War general was shocked at the conditions at Bosque Redondo. He decided to move the Navajos to a reservation in Indian Territory (Oklahoma) or Texas. Barboncito, one of the headmen, made a strong plea to allow the Navajos to return to Dinetah. Sherman agreed, and a treaty was made that set up a reservation there.

A group of headmen signed the treaty on June 1, 1868. They agreed to stop raiding, to remain at peace, and to send Navajo children to schools run by white people. The U.S. government agreed to supply the Navajos with sheep, goats, cattle, farming equipment, and seeds.

The Navajo reservation was established in what is now northeastern Arizona and northwestern New Mexico. It was much smaller than the original Dinetah, but at least it was located where some of the Navajos had been living before the Long Walk. Most other Native Americans were placed on very small reservations far from their original homes.

The Navajo Nation is nearly as large as the state of West Virginia.

Only one-half of the Navajo people had survived the Place of Despair. When the people returned to their land, life was still very difficult. Hogans and peach orchards had been destroyed. Food and clothing were very scarce. Gradually Navajos began to rebuild their herds of animals.

In 1882 the Navajos had another setback. The government established a reservation for the Hopi

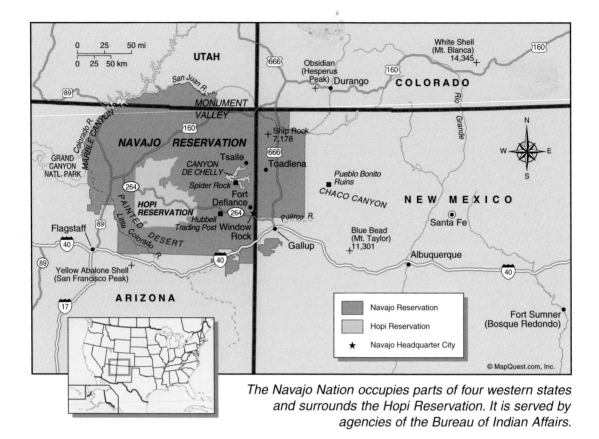

The Navajo Nation occupies parts of four western states and surrounds the Hopi Reservation. It is served by agencies of the Bureau of Indian Affairs.

Indians on part of the land that the Navajos claimed as theirs. This was the beginning of a land dispute that continues today.

Growth and Change

The 1880s was a period of growth for the Navajos. The number of people and the size of the animal herds increased. By the 1890s, overgrazing was becoming a problem in some areas. Sheep, cattle, and horses were eating grass faster than it could grow back. The land began to erode, topsoil was carried away, and **gullies** formed. Plants will not grow on such barren ground, and erosion continued.

Navajo culture was also changing. The **Bureau of Indian Affairs (BIA)** set up schools on the reservation. Most teaching was aimed at turning Navajo students into "good Americans." Children were sent to **boarding schools** away from their families.

Punishments were very harsh. No one was allowed to speak the Navajo language. Diné traditions and values were ignored.

Stock Reduction

The Great Depression, which began in 1929, led to low prices for livestock products. By 1931 the BIA had decided that the size of the Navajo sheep herds had to be reduced to control overgrazing of the land.

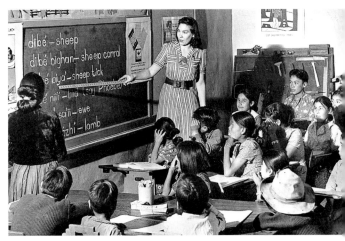

A group of Navajo children in 1948 studying English for the first time.

The Navajos were strongly opposed to the stock reduction plan, but at first they surrendered their livestock voluntarily. And they knew that their animals were at least being used to feed people elsewhere in the country. By the end of the program in the 1940s, however, sheep and horses were being taken from their owners by force and shot on the spot. The dead livestock was left to rot and fed no one at all. Angry Navajos viewed the slaughter as an attack on their culture. They compared this cruel waste of life to Bosque Redondo and again felt betrayed by the U.S. government.

After the stock reduction program, Navajo people could no longer depend completely on animals to support their families. Some people began to work at government jobs on the reservation or in nearby towns. These jobs included drilling water wells and building windmills. A hospital and 43 day schools were built. Trees and grass were replanted on overgrazed land. Other people began to work for ranches and private businesses off the reservation.

Way of Life

Throughout their whole history, the Diné have learned from other cultures, taking useful ideas, changing them, and making them their own. The ideas that had the greatest importance for Navajo culture were growing corn and raising sheep.

Corn became the main food for the Diné. The importance of this grain in their diet is reflected by its importance in religious life. Corn pollen is used in healing and blessing ceremonies. **Traditional** people carry corn pollen in a pouch. In their prayers they offer corn pollen to Mother Earth and Sun, to water, and to each new day. Corn is so significant in Navajo life that the design of a growing cornstalk is used to symbolize the Navajo people.

Holy People stand with cornstalks in a wall hanging of woven cloth.

The Diné acquired domestic animals from the Spaniards, who brought horses, cattle, sheep, and goats to New Mexico. Horses allowed the Navajos to hunt, travel, and raid easily. But sheep became even more valuable. By the late 1700s, sheep were at the center of Navajo life. Families began to rely on sheep for meat. They learned to spin wool and to weave the yarn into clothes, blankets, and rugs.

A successful family had many sheep. The flocks were moved from camp to camp, according to the season, for better grazing. Everyone in the family had a job to do. Children often watched over sheep, and dogs were used to protect the flock from coyotes. The size of the flock was maintained and increased with the lambs born each spring. Later in the spring, the sheep were shorn, and the wool was prepared for weaving. Extra wool and woven blankets not needed by the family could be taken to a **trading post**, a special type of store on the reservation where wool and woven items could be sold or exchanged for other goods. Sheep became so important to the culture of the Navajo that some say "Sheep are life."

Food

The meat of sheep (called mutton) and goats is an important part of the Navajo diet. Some families also eat beef and pork. A few families keep chickens as well for their eggs and meat. Fruit and melons are also grown. Corn is eaten in many dishes, and ground cornmeal is used to bake bread for ceremonies.

Many families now have replaced cornmeal with white flour from supermarkets for everyday use, even for fry bread. To prepare this favorite Navajo recipe, the cook deep-fries the dough quickly in hot oil. Navajo tacos, made with fry bread rather than tortillas, is a popular dish, as is mutton stew.

Traditionally, Navajo families relied on sheep raising and shearing for a large part of their income.

A Navajo girl plays with her family's lambs. Now pets, later they will be valuable resources for her family.

Hogans

The traditional housing of the Diné is the hogan. Its shape resembles the **hide** dwellings of the Athapaskans. A hogan is a round, six-sided or eight-sided shelter. The walls are wood or logs covered with tree bark, mud, or adobe (sun-dried earth). These natural materials provide good insulation and keep hogans cool in the summer and warm in the winter. Inside, there is a stove or hearth in the center and a smoke hole in the roof.

A hole in the hogan's roof lets smoke from the cooking and heating fire escape.

Hogans are located in relation to the four directions. Traditionally, a stone from each of the four sacred mountains is used in the foundation. The doorway always faces east, so people can greet the rising sun. Women sit on the south side, and men sit on the north side. One enters and moves in a clockwise direction.

Today many people live in other types of houses, but they may have a hogan nearby to use for ceremonies. People live

The hogan is a traditional Navajo dwelling. Its doorway faces east, and the roof is covered with mud for warmth in the winter and cooling in the summer.

near relatives in a compound (a group of houses or hogans) so they can work together. Also, there are now about two dozen small towns scattered across the reservation.

Navajo families build a shade house of branches to use on hot summer days.

Clothing

After they moved to the desert, the Diné adopted loose-fitting clothing like their Pueblo neighbors. Men wore pants made of buckskin or cloth with silver buttons down the side. Women wore wool dresses made of two blankets stitched at the shoulders and sides. They sometimes used a belt of cloth.

In the 1870s, Navajo men began to wear long shirts of **velveteen** or calico and pants made of cotton with a belt of silver. The women wore long, full cotton skirts and velveteen blouses. Blankets from the trading posts were used to keep warm. Jewelry, especially silver and **turquoise**, was worn on special occasions as a sign of wealth. Some present-day Navajos wear traditional clothing most of the time. Others wear the ordinary clothing found anywhere in

Traditional Navajos looked stately in their beautiful woolen blankets, which they often wore like coats in cold weather.

the Southwest for everyday occasions and save their traditional clothing for special events and ceremonies.

The traditional hairstyle, the *tsiyeeł*, is worn by both men and women. Hair is parted in the center, pulled back, twisted into a **figure eight**, and wrapped with string or yarn. Men may wear headbands, especially during ceremonies.

Arts and Crafts

Traditional stories say that most Navajo arts and crafts are gifts from the Holy People. For example, one story tells how Spider Woman taught women of the Diné how to weave, and

In a trading post on the Navajo reservation, the sale of brightly colored, hand-woven rugs has been a source of income for generations.

the **loom** was built according to directions given by Spider Man. By the late 1500s, Navajo women had begun to spin wool and to be recognized as skilled weavers. This skill was passed from mother to daughter.

In the 1870s, Navajo weavers started making rugs rather than blankets. Some of the colors and some designs were changed to appeal to the people in the East. The weavers, however, always kept their own style and creativity. Patterns are named according to the location where they are woven. Popular rug patterns now are geometric designs, such as Two Grey Hills or Ganado, and designs with figures, such as the Tree of Life from the northwestern part of the reservation.

Some designs and symbols show sacred images. Weavers sing certain songs as they work. They believe this helps them to avoid mistakes and conflict in the designs and makes their weaving harmonious. Weavers and their art reflect the Navajo concept of beauty and craftsmanship. Navajo weaving is recognized around the world for its excellence.

Navajo men learned to work with silver from Mexican **smiths** in the 1850s. As a part of the treaty of 1868 that set up the Navajo reservation, the U.S. government agreed to send silver-working tools to the Navajos. They began to make buttons, necklaces, rings, bracelets, earrings, belts, and ornaments for horses. Turquoise, a local stone representing the well-being of the individual, was added to jewelry designs in about 1880. Navajos wore this jewelry on special occasions. Traders encouraged the silversmiths to make pieces to sell or trade. The silver and turquoise jewelry of Navajo craftspeople is recognized today for its unique beauty.

Vivid designs tightly woven on hand looms are treasured the world over as among the finest examples of fabric making.

After the tribe returned from Bosque Redondo, trading posts became an important part of traditional Navajo life. The white traders provided cotton cloth, coffee, flour, and cookware in return for wool and crafts. The traders encouraged the making of jewelry and weaving to sell to travelers coming west on the railroads. Some traders tried to cheat the Navajos, but many were honest and tried to learn their language.

Tradition says that First Man and First Woman made baskets, with each part having a special meaning, to be used in the ceremonies. Navajos produced baskets and pottery for their personal and family use. In the late 1960s, the Navajo Community College began to encourage craftspeople to produce baskets and pottery to sell. Today Navajo craftspeople produce beautiful weaving, silver jewelry, pottery, baskets, folk art animal carvings, and **sandpaintings**. There are also many talented Navajo artists and sculptors.

Navajo silversmiths and turquoise jewelry makers are famous for their designs and craftsmanship.

Pottery and sandpaintings are distinctively Navajo.

A young Navajo woman flashes a smile as bright and lively as her fine necklaces.

Religion—The Beauty Way

The religion of the Diné is their way of life. In the creation story, the Holy People designed the land to be a happy, healthy, and harmonious place and taught the Diné how to live the right way. Navajo spiritual life is a search for the state of hózhó, which is sometimes translated into English as "the Beauty Way." Hózhó is harmony, beauty, order, balance—everything that is good for people. Hózhó exists within a person, between a person and others, and also between a person and the Holy People. An important part of hózhó is respect for Mother Earth. She provides for her children, and all must honor her.

In the beginning, the Holy People taught the healing and blessing ceremonies to the Diné. There are more than 50 ceremonies. They help people return to hózhó, cure sickness, bless a new home or marriage, and to protect families, herds, and crops. A ceremony is led by a **hataałi** (HA tal ee), or singer. This person has memorized the complex songs and prayers that attract the attention of the Holy People.

A Nockideneh family rug woven in the Tree of Life pattern

25

Dancers celebrating the winter Yeibeichai, or Nightway, ceremony

Besides the songs, a ceremony includes sandpainting, some-times called drypainting. An elaborate design is worked out on the ground, using not paint but colored earth, pollen, charcoal, cornmeal, crushed flowers, and sand. Sandpaintings often show the Holy People and remind participants of the stories connected with them. The person for whom the ceremony is being held sits on the painting to receive power or healing from the Holy People. At the end of the ceremony, the painting is rubbed out, and the sand is carried outside toward the east. Sage, corn pollen, certain herbs, and the soap from the **yucca** plant are also used in ceremonies.

Some ceremonies last only a few hours, and others last as long as nine days. The Yeibeichai, or Nightway, ceremony is conducted in the winter, while the Squaw Dance, or Enemyway, is held in the summer.

A favorite ceremony to promote hózhó is the Baby Laughing Feast, held when a baby first laughs. The parents act as if the baby is the host of the feast and the giver of the gifts. By this ceremony of hospitality, the family expresses its hope that the baby will be generous through his or her whole life.

Children become recognized members of the Diné during a part of the Yeibeichai ceremony. Children are given their sacred names at that time. This name remains a secret, rarely shared with others and never mentioned casually.

Kinaalda, which honors Changing Woman, is the four-day ceremony for girls who have reached maturity. Navajo girls are given advice and instruction by older women on how they should behave as adults. Each day for four days girls wake up before dawn and run toward the rising sun to symbolize following in the footsteps of all women. They are massaged each day to make them strong. On the last day, they host a special feast and give blessings to those who attend. There is no similar ceremony for boys.

An important Navajo ritual is the use of the sweat lodge. This structure is a smaller version of the old-style hogan without the smoke hole. Rocks are heated outside. They are brought inside, and water is poured on them to produce steam. The Holy People are invited to join in the sweat bath. Songs are sung, and prayers are offered. The sweat house is a place to cleanse the body and the mind.

Young girl wearing a traditional Navajo dress

The number four is very significant and is found throughout Navajo culture and religion. There are four directions, four seasons, four original clans, and four colors associated with the four sacred mountains. Most ceremonies consist of four songs or multiples of four songs.

The early Spanish missionaries were unsuccessful in converting the Diné to Christianity. At present, Navajos who follow the religious ways of the Diné are called Traditionals. Other Navajos belong to Mormon, Catholic, and Protestant churches, although many also participate in traditional ceremonies on appropriate occasions. Other Navajos are members of the Native American Church, where worship combines both Christian and Indian practices.

Window Rock, a rock formation where sacred ceremonies are held, gives its name to the capital of the Navajo Nation.

Family Life

Clans

Navajo society and family life revolve around the clan system. A clan is a group of people who are related to each other. Hundreds of people can belong to a single clan. Four of the oldest clans are Bitter Water, Towering House, Salt People, and Edge Water. Over the years new clans have formed, and today there are about 60. Some have the names of places, such as Coyote Pass, Honeycombed Rock, and Where the Waters Join. Other new clans (Zia, Zuni, San Felipe) formed when non-Navajo people married into the tribe.

The Diné introduce themselves by name and tell their clans. A person is born for his mother's clan and born to his father's clan. Someone might be born for Bitter Water and born to Salt People. Both boys and girls are born into their mother's clan and trace their relations this way, which makes the Diné a **matrilineal** society. A person may not marry a member of his or her own clan (mother's) or a member of his or her father's clan.

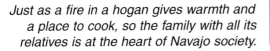

Just as a fire in a hogan gives warmth and a place to cook, so the family with all its relatives is at the heart of Navajo society.

29

Children

Babies are very valued members of the family and usually the center of attention. They may spend much of their first two years in a cradleboard, a portable bed made of wood. A baby is wrapped in cloth or a blanket and strapped onto the board with pieces of leather. The baby can be easily carried in a cradleboard by parents while they are working.

Young Navajos learn by example from watching others and listening to their grandparents. For all children, the extended family of grandparents, aunts, uncles, and cousins is very important.

Navajos value hard work and reliability. A person should have freedom, but it is important to cooperate with others and help friends and family. Respect for the land and all living creatures is also part of being a Navajo. Above all, a person should walk the Beauty Way. Hózhó (page 25) means balance and harmony and is the ideal for family life. If a person misbehaves, that reflects badly on the entire family. One of the worst things that can be said to someone is: "You act as if you have no relatives."

Children are expected to help their elders and to contribute to the family by doing a share of the work. Caring for sheep helps teach children to pay attention to the world around them and to be responsible. Lambs, given as gifts, are the beginning of a young person's flock.

Infants in cradleboards and young children are at the center of family life. As they grow, they will help with chores and learn responsibility.

Happy Times

Navajo language arts are very rich. Conversations are full of humor and word plays, or puns, because the language is so complex. People also enjoy telling stories during the winter, especially tales of Coyote, the Trickster.

Several games are popular among the Navajos. It is said that the shoe game was invented by Coyote to settle a disagreement among the animals. This game is played in the winter months by the night animal team and the day animal team. One team hides a ball in a shoe and fills it with sand. Four shoes are buried in a pile of earth. The other team has to guess which shoe the ball is in.

Like children everywhere, Navajo children enjoy playing string games. The strings are held in the hands, worked into loops, and wrapped around the fingers. The simplest pattern is called "the bird's nest" or "tea cup and saucer." Some of the more complex patterns show the constellations in the night sky, and some show designs used in Navajo rugs.

The fancy patterns children create in string games (below) may end up in designs of woven blankets (right).

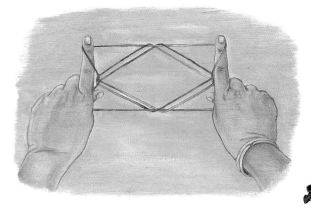

Tribal Government

The Diné began to think of themselves as a tribe and a nation only in recent times. Originally, they were a collection of clans bound together only by language, religion, and way of life. There was no chief of all the people, but sometimes a local leader, or headman, would lead a group of warriors into battle or on a raid.

Dealing with the Diné was a problem for the U.S. government. Several headmen signed the 1868 treaty, but this bound only the signers and their families. For example, a headman who received food as promised by the treaty would distribute it to his relatives only. The government, however, had intended for this food to go to a large group of people.

In 1921 oil was discovered on the reservation. At the time the Navajos lived in compounds scattered across the reservation, and no organized group had the power to agree to leasing the land. With the encouragement of the Bureau of

The Tribal Council Chambers building at Window Rock, Arizona, is built in the shape of a hogan.

Indian Affairs, the first Navajo Tribal Council met in Toadlena, New Mexico, on July 27, 1923. Chee Dodge, a prominent leader, was elected tribal chairman by the twelve delegates. This council made an important decision. The money from the oil leases would go into a tribal fund rather than be divided so that each Navajo received a small share. Since that time lease money has been used to improve the entire Navajo Nation.

In 1969 the Navajo Nation officially came into being, with headquarters at Window Rock, Arizona. It is now governed by a Tribal Council made up of a chairman, vice chairman, and 88 delegates. The Council meets at least four times a year to discuss critical issues and make laws. The tribal government works through five administrative areas, which are further divided into 110 **chapters** that settle local issues, such as livestock permits. A police force and a court system are also part of the tribal government.

Electricity, gas, water, and sewage on the reservation are controlled by the Navajo Tribal Utility Authority. The Navajo Housing Authority creates and maintains adequate housing. Funds for preschools, legal aid, drug and alcohol treatment programs, and other community services are provided by the Office of Navajo Economic Opportunities. The Navajo Nation also publishes a weekly newspaper, *The Navajo Times.*

The Tribal Council meets at Window Rock, Arizona, to discuss the future of the Navajo Nation.

Contemporary Life

World War II

World War II brought many changes to the lives of the Diné. Despite hard feelings caused by the stock reduction program (see page 17), Navajos knew their country was under attack and wanted to defend it. Navajos served with honor in operations against the Germans and Italians in Europe and the Japanese in the Pacific. About 3,600 served in the armed forces, and about 10,000 civilians were involved in war work on and off the reservation.

The Navajo language was used as a secret code during World War II.

Early in the war, a U.S. Marine officer, Philip Johnson, who had grown up on the reservation, developed the idea of using the Navajo language to send messages on the battlefield by radio. The Code Talkers were a special unit of more than 400 Marines who developed a code using their very complex language. This code was so effective that it was the only one the Japanese could not break during World War II. The Code Talkers served in the front lines as the Marines fought their way from island to island in the Pacific.

Changes in Reservation Life

When the war ended, thousands of service men and women and war workers returned to the reservation. The stock reduction program had continued during the war, and the smaller flocks of sheep could not support a family. Few jobs were available on the reservation. Many people had to leave in order to find work in cities. People were no longer living with their families, and children could not be raised in the traditional way.

In 1950 Congress passed the Navajo-Hopi Rehabilitation Act. Its purpose was to enable Navajos and Hopis to take charge of their own reservations and to provide funding for improvements in roads, health care, and schools.

Newly paved roads meant that the Navajos did not have to rely on their nearby trading posts, which usually had high prices. They could easily go off the reservation to shop. Better roads also brought more tourists onto the reservation, which created more jobs.

Education

Many of the soldiers who served in World War II spoke little or no English and could not read or write. They had to go to special schools to learn military commands. Those veterans came home convinced that education was important for the future.

A few state public schools were started on the reservation. But thousands of children had to live away from home in BIA boarding schools. Fortunately, two trends in the 1950s helped solve this problem. More people moved to towns and therefore

Summer school is a lot cooler and a lot more fun outdoors with a breeze and shade at lunchtime.

The hogan-shaped Ned A. Hatathli Cultural Center, part of Diné College in Tsaile, Arizona, offers many cultural and educational opportunities.

lived closer to schools. Their children did not have to board away from home. And in rural areas better roads meant children could ride buses to attend public or day schools.

Navajo parents became more involved in their children's education. They wanted the Navajo language, history, and culture to be at the center of what the schools taught. Educational materials that used traditional stories and values were developed. In Rough Rock, a demonstration school was established to show how education could be improved in the Navajo way.

In 1968 the Tribal Council founded the Navajo Community College (recently renamed Diné College) now located in Tsaile, Arizona. This was the first Indian-owned community college in the country. The cultural center, which features arts and crafts of the Navajo people, is a six-story hogan-shaped building. The usual college subjects are taught along with weaving, pottery, basketry, and silversmithing. Other courses focus on training people to teach the Navajo language and culture.

Traditional dyes, patience, memory, skill, and spirit go into the finest weaving.

Economic Development

Many families continue to have small herds of sheep and other animals. Sheep are still herded with dogs, but now all-terrain vehicles (ATVs) sometimes take the place of horses.

Weaving is still an important source of income for some families. Weavers may sell their rugs at trading posts or in urban areas. Chapter houses have started programs where women are paid wages to weave. The rugs are then sold at **auction**. The Navajo Nation has also established shops on the reservation where arts and crafts are sold.

Beginning in the 1950s, oil, uranium, and coal **leases** brought money from outside companies and some jobs onto the reservation. However, development of these minerals was sometimes damaging to the land and to the Navajo people. For example, coal was strip-mined, which means that layers of earth are removed to expose the coal. Once the coal is removed, the pit remains, and the land is scarred and unusable. Other coal-mining practices caused pollution, and the tribe had to sue the coal companies to stop.

Pollution was also caused by power plants that burn coal to produce electricity. On the positive side, power plants provided jobs on the reservation and produced electricity for Navajo people to use and to sell to outside areas.

Nuclear energy was another example of damaging development. Navajos worked in the uranium mines without the protection that should have been provided for their safety. Many miners developed lung cancer years later and were finally given some money by the U.S. government. The largest nuclear accident in

Opened in 1871, Hubbell Trading Post still does business today. It is a favorite stopping place for visitors.

A farm at the bottom of Canyon de Chelly uses dry farming to grow crops.

U.S. history occurred in 1979, when millions of gallons of water contaminated by **radioactive** wastes were released into the Puerco River, a river near Church Rock, New Mexico. Livestock near the river became ill and died. The water and land along the river cannot be used for decades to come. This was a terrible environmental disaster.

Mineral development brought a few other disappointments. Some U.S. government agents and a few Navajo leaders used their positions for personal gain. In other cases, industries were encouraged to locate on the reservation but did not bring as many jobs as had been hoped.

Nevertheless, the natural resources of the Navajo reservation are a big economic advantage. In addition to minerals, many acres of the reservation are covered with commercial timber, and there are also areas of rich farming land. Careful conservation and wise management of these resources will benefit Navajos both today and in the future.

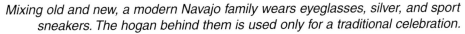

Navajo-Hopi Lands

Mineral resources played a part in the unsettled problem of Navajo and Hopi reservation borders. After World War II, the Hopis wanted to gain complete ownership of the disputed lands. Most Navajos believed that the Hopis did not intend to use the land themselves but expected to profit because coal and oil companies wanted to develop the area. In 1974 Congress attempted to solve the land disagreement by dividing the disputed lands into two equal parts, the Navajo Partition Land (NPL) and the Hopi Partition Land (HPL).

Some 100 Hopis lived on the NPL, but about 10,000 Navajos lived on the HPL and had for many generations. These people were relocated, meaning they had to move away to another area. Most went to towns on or off the reservation. The Navajo Tribal Council fought this relocation in Congress and in the courts but did not succeed.

Mixing old and new, a modern Navajo family wears eyeglasses, silver, and sport sneakers. The hogan behind them is used only for a traditional celebration.

Thousands of people were moved, some by force. This move was sometimes called the Second Long Walk. Relocation pushed traditional people into another world, completely removing them from the land and their way of life. Dishonest real estate agents and loan officers took advantage of people who were unfamiliar with the world of taxes, mortgages, and utility bills. The deadline for relocation to be completed was 1986, but in 1997 there were still a few Navajos living in the HPL. This dispute caused much sadness and many bad feelings that will last for years.

Outlook for the Future

Today there are more than 200,000 Navajos. Some have moved to cities to find jobs, but most live on the reservation, which covers 17.5 million acres (7 million ha) in Arizona and New Mexico. Income on the reservation is low, and many people are very poor because they cannot find jobs. Some people have health problems because of poor diet. Some cannot

Wheatfields Lake is one of the recreation areas on the reservation where people can fish, boat, and camp.

A rodeo at a Fourth of July celebration offers Navajo cowboys a chance to show off their skills and win prize money.

obtain good medical care. A reliable supply of water is also a problem in certain areas. Drugs, alcoholism, and traffic accidents are problems on the reservation just as they are throughout the United States.

The Navajo Nation is trying to develop tourism. The reservation—or Navajoland as it is called—is very beautiful country, and offers many things for visitors to do. More than 20 lakes and reservoirs provide fishing. Other areas have campgrounds. The largest Native American fair in the world is the annual Navajo Tribal Fair at Window Rock. This weeklong event, held every September, includes dances, horse racing, a rodeo, arts and crafts demonstrations and sales, produce and livestock exhibits, a fry bread contest, and the Miss Navajo pageant. The spectacular desert scenery of Dinetah is world famous. The Ship Rock is a large volcanic formation that was, according to legend, the home of the Bird Monster and the heart of Mother Earth. Monument Valley, with its interesting rock formations, **mesas**, and **buttes**, has been the setting of many Hollywood movies.

Also in Navajoland lie ruins of ancient villages that were inhabited by the Anasazi people who moved from the area about 700 to 900

Navajo dancers compete in a local dance contest.

years ago. Pueblo Bonito in Chaco Canyon is one of the largest. Other ruins are found in Canyon de Chelly and in Kinlichee.

The Navajo Nation is trying to develop a strong economy and create new jobs. At the same time, all Navajos are committed to keeping true to their distinct culture. The Diné are very proud of their history and especially proud of who they are. The Navajo language is spoken and used everywhere. An outsider may see poverty or lack of material things in some places, but the Navajo way of life is rich and full. Everything Navajos do is linked to the past of the people. They try to appreciate life with each new day and respect the Earth and all its creatures. The family remains at the center of their culture. Above all, the Diné continue to strive for hózhó—balance, harmony, and beauty in their lives.

Navajo children learn from and greatly respect their elders.

Navajo Recipes

Navajo Fry Bread

Adult supervision is required.

2 quarts vegetable oil or lard
3 cups flour
1 tablespoon baking powder
$\frac{1}{2}$ teaspoon salt
1 cup warm water

Fry bread cooking on an open fire.

Heat the lard or oil in a deep pot or heavy skillet.

Mix the flour, baking powder, and salt in a large mixing bowl.

Add warm water in small amounts, and knead the dough until it is soft but not sticky. Sometimes more flour or more water will need to be added. Cover the bowl, and let it sit for 15 minutes.

Take an egg-sized ball of dough and roll or pat it into a round disk about $\frac{1}{4}$-inch thick. Punch a hole in the center, and pierce the dough several times with a fork. This allows the dough to puff up when frying.

Drop into the pot, and fry until golden brown. If using a skillet, fry on one side until bubbles appear and then turn over and fry until golden brown.

Navajo Taco

Place layers of shredded lettuce, diced tomatoes, chopped onions, and fried hamburger on the prepared fry bread. Top with red or green chili sauce, and fold over.

Navajo Prayer

Hóshóogo naasháá doo	In beauty I walk
Shitsiji' hózhóogo naasháa doo	With beauty before me I walk
Shikéédéé' hózhóogo naasháa doo	With beauty behind me I walk
Shideigi hózhóogo naasháa doo	With beauty above me I walk
T'áá altso shinaagóó hózhóogo naasháá doo	With beauty around me I walk
Hózhó náhásdlii'	It has become beauty again
Hózhó náhásdlii'	It has become beauty again
Hózhó náhásdlii'	It has become beauty again
Hózhó náhásdlii'	It has become beauty again

Further Reading

Aaseng, Nathan. *Navajo Code Talkers*. New York: Walker and Co., 1992.

Iverson, Peter. *The Navajos*. New York: Chelsea House Publishers, 1990.

Newcomb, Franc Johnson. *Navajo Folk Tales*. Albuquerque: University of New Mexico Press, 1967.

Nies, Judith. *Native American History*. New York: Ballantine Books, 1996.

Page, Susanne, and Jake Page. *Navajo*. New York: Harry N. Abrams, 1995.

Navajo Chronology

825–1000	Athapaskan people migrate from Alaska to the Southwest.
1582	Diné first encounter Spanish explorers near Mt. Taylor.
1600–1800s	Spanish and New Mexicans kidnap Navajos for use as slaves.
1620s	Navajos obtain horses from Spanish.
1692	Navajos accept Pueblo refugees from Spanish oppression.
1849	Murder of Narbona and other Navajos by U.S. Army
1851	Fort Defiance is built. It is the first permanent presence of U.S. government in Dinetah.
1861	Fort Fauntleroy massacre
1863	General James Carleton orders Colonel Kit Carson to forcibly remove Navajos from their homeland.
1864	Long Walk to Bosque Redondo (Ft. Sumner)
1868	Headmen sign treaty setting up a reservation for the Navajo.
1882	Hopi reservation is established.
1922	Oil is discovered on the Navajo reservation.
1923	First Tribal Council is formed.
1933–1944	Stock Reduction Act results in destruction of 250,000 animals.
1942–1945	3,600 Navajos serve in armed services, 420 as Marine Code Talkers
1947	Mineral survey finds deposits of uranium, coal, oil, and natural gas on reservation.
1951	Uranium mining begins. Unprotected workers later suffer much illness.
1956–1958	First attempt to settle the Navajo-Hopi land dispute
1969	Navajo Nation officially formed
1974	Navajo Relocation Act—12,000 from Hopi Partition Land Peabody Coal opens strip mine in area.
1979	Puerco River nuclear accident, largest in U.S. history
1996	Navajos successfully sue Peabody Coal to stop pollution.

Glossary

Anasazi The prehistoric inhabitants of the canyons of northern Arizona and New Mexico and southwestern Colorado.

Auction The sale of goods to the highest bidder.

Boarding school A school where children live, receiving meals and a place to sleep.

Bureau of Indian Affairs (BIA) The agency that carries out U.S. government laws, treaties, and policies related to American Indians.

Butte A hill with a flat top and steep sides.

Ceremony A religious rite used to mark a special occasion. Navajos, for example, had a ceremony for healing or for the first laugh of a child.

Chapter The lowest level of Navajo tribal government.

Clan A group of people related to each other.

Diné "The People," the Navajo's name for themselves.

Figure eight A design formed as a continuous line that crosses itself making two loops, such as the numeral 8.

Gully A trench worn in the earth by running water.

Hataałi A person who conducts ceremonies for healing or blessing, also called a singer.

Headman The leader of a small local group of Navajo families.

Hide The skin of an animal. Some hides are cleaned and tanned to make leather.

Hogan The traditional Navajo round, 6-sided, or 8-sided house built of wood and mud or adobe.

Holy People The supernatural beings who gave the pattern of life for all creatures. Navajos believe they are part of the ceremonies that restore hózhó in the lives of the Diné.

Hózhó Harmony, order, balance, beauty; everything that is good for people.

Lease A written agreement that allows the use of land for a certain purpose for a certain period of time.

Loom A frame for weaving thread or yarn to make cloth.

Matrilineal Determining family relationships through the mother's clan.

Mesa A flat-topped, steep-sided land formation with a bigger area than a butte.

Missionary One whose work is convincing others to accept his or her religion.

Pueblo Native peoples of the Southwest who live in villages with flat-roofed stone or adobe houses; neighbors of the Navajo.

Radioactive Giving off energy in particles or waves as the nuclei (central points) of atoms change.

Sandpainting (drypainting) A complex design created by the careful placement of small particles of colored earth, pollen, charcoal, cornmeal, crushed flowers, and sand. Sandpaintings often show the Holy People or parts of the Navajo creation story, and they are used in healing and blessing ceremonies.

Smallpox A very contagious disease, often deadly, caused by a virus. A person with smallpox has a high fever and pus-filled bumps on the skin that can leave deep, permanent scars.

Smith One who works metal.

Sweat lodge A small building where people cleanse and purify themselves in heat from steam.

Trading post A special type of store where goods can be exchanged for other goods.

Traditional The old ways, or a person who follows the customs of his or her ancestors.

Travois A device used to carry loads consisting of a platform or net between two poles dragged by dogs or horses.

Treaty An agreement made by two sides.

Turquoise A stone with a blue-green color often used in jewelry.

Velveteen Cotton fabric that imitates velvet.

Yucca A plant native to warm regions of the Americas with sword-shaped leaves and white, waxy flowers.

Index

Numbers in italics indicate illustration or map.